D1104483

Everything
You Need to
Know About Compulsive

Sexual

Behavior

A single-minded fascination with sex prevents some individuals from experiencing real feelings with real people.

Everything You Need to Know About Compulsive Sexual Behavior

Laura Gilbert

The Rosen Publishing Group, Inc.
New York

Published in 2001 by The Rosen Publishing Group, Inc.
29 East 21st Street, New York, NY 10010

First Edition

Library of Congress Cataloging-in-Publication Data

Gilbert, Laura, 1976–
    Everything you need to know about compulsive sexual behavior / by Laura Gilbert—1st ed.
        p. cm. — (The need to know library)
Includes bibliographical references and index.
Summary: Defines compulsive sexual behavior in teenagers and how it differs from the norm, discusses how it develops, and presents some of the methods available to treat the problem.
    ISBN 0-8239-3290-7
    1. Sex addiction—Juvenile literature. [1. Sex addiction. 2. Youth—Sexual behavior. 3. Sexual ethics.] I. Title. II. Series.
    RC560.S43 .G44 2000
    616.85'83—dc21

                                                00-009003

Manufactured in the United States of America

83649

Contents

Curiosity about sex leads some teens to look at pornographic materials.

Introduction

As young people go through puberty, their hormones surge and their interest in sex spikes. Many young people spend a lot of time fantasizing about romantic relationships and thinking about sex. For some teens, curiosity about sex leads them to look at pornographic materials, whether magazines or movies. Masturbation, or self-stimulatory behavior, is very common among teens.

All of these are normal responses to the changes that go on in the teenage mind. For the first time, young people are experiencing adult sexual urges. They are also surrounded by other kids going through the same things, as well as a culture that is obsessed with sex.

Most teens will, over the next few years, experience various phases of sex and love. Eventually they will learn to form real relationships and, ultimately, sexual relationships. Their single-minded fascination with sex will shrink to be just one part of a full, adult life that includes friendships, romance, work, hobbies, recreation, and perhaps religion.

But for a handful of individuals, this development never happens. Instead of learning how to deal with other people, they turn to sexual behavior as a substitute for real feelings and real people. As they watch others successfully settle down, they feel alone, worthless, and alienated. Their sexual behavior becomes a source of embarrassment. Because it is the only way they know how to process certain feelings, it becomes a main focus of their daily lives. Soon, the behavior is controlling them—they can't explain it, but they can't stop it.

This kind of psychological problem is referred to as a sexual compulsion or sexual addiction. It is not common, but it can be very damaging. People with this disorder are powerless to stop their activity, even if it ruins their friendships, relationships, careers, and finances. Some may have their spouses leave them; others may even wind up in jail.

Who are these people and how does the problem develop? This book discusses compulsive sexual behavior—the reasons behind it and ways to treat it. You will also learn about the types and degree of sexual activity that are considered "normal" and what to do if you are concerned about your own behavior or the behavior of a friend or family member.

Chapter One

Out of Control

In the stories below, you will read about teens whose sexual behavior is disturbing, but who seem perfectly normal to those around them. They are popular, have lots of friends, come from stable families, are involved with school activities, and seem relatively happy. Their unhealthy sexual behavior is only one aspect of their lives, and they may go to great lengths to hide it from the people around them. Perhaps one of them reminds you of a friend of yours—or perhaps their stories reflect something going on in your own life.

For sixteen-year-old Matt, masturbation isn't just part of his daily routine—it defines it. Though he knows that practically everyone his age does it—some people even more than he does— Matt finds himself constantly obsessing over his next experience. When his busy schedule and big family don't afford him the privacy to masturbate three times a day, he finds himself getting agitated and angry. Lately, he has even started doing it in the school bathroom or in a closet at work, just to make sure that he gets the release he needs. Afterward he feels ashamed and guilty for doing it in a public place. He promises himself that he won't do it again but soon finds himself repeating the behavior. Matt wishes he knew how to stop, but is too ashamed to ask for help.

Lisa, a freshman in high school, has been dating different guys since she was twelve. What started as a puppy-love relationship in junior high soon became everything to Lisa. When her boyfriend broke up with her suddenly, Lisa felt confused and depressed. That night, she went out with some friends to a party and slept with a guy she had just met to make herself feel better. Since that time, Lisa has bounced from boyfriend to boyfriend, often going to bed with older men in the hopes of keeping them interested. Living without a boyfriend is unimaginable to Lisa—she has never gone more than a couple of days between cutting things off with one guy and finding a new one.

Andrew was fourteen when his family got an Internet connection at home. When he was sure that his parents weren't around, Andrew looked up a few porn sites. Soon he was coming home every day to surf pornographic sites, saving particular images on floppy disks. Three years later, Andrew feels controlled by his porn habit. He has over fifteen disks stored in a shoebox under his bed, filled to capacity with pictures of nude women. Every few months he grows disgusted with his collection and throws the disks away—only to find himself buying a new box of empty disks a week or two later. Andrew spends at least an hour a day at his favorite Web sites. He rarely socializes after school, preferring instead to use the time before his parents get off work to go home and look at porn.

Ever since seventeen-year-old Angie started having sexual thoughts, she has always imagined herself in situations where she's nude in public. The thought of flashing an unsuspecting stranger turns Angie on—and also makes her feel like a weirdo. Every few months, her desire to expose herself becomes uncontrollable. Twice in the last year, Angie has gone to the mall wearing a skirt with no underwear, taking the escalator in front of older men in the hopes that they'll glance up.

Growing up, thirteen-year-old Mike's bedroom window faced an apartment complex next door. He *would occasionally peek through his window to watch women undressing or couples being intimate. When he was eleven, he began masturbating as he watched certain people in their apartments. Now he can satisfy his urges only by fantasizing that he is watching someone who doesn't know it. He has even found himself wondering how he can get away with spying on people he knows—plotting out where they live, when they go to bed, how he can get to their house. Though he has never actually done anything about it, Mike is afraid he might one day act on his Peeping Tom fantasies—and get caught.*

Ann Marie is an honors student about to graduate. Between college applications and advanced classes, she has had a stressful year. She and her long-term boyfriend have sex several times a week, but Ann Marie still fantasizes nonstop about other guys she knows. When she is having a particularly grueling week, she often calls her ex-boyfriend, and the two fool around in private. Once, when both her boyfriend and her ex-boyfriend were out of town, Ann Marie, upset over a poor test score, called an attractive friend and asked him to come over. They ended up having sex. Her boyfriend has no idea that Ann Marie is cheating on him. Ann Marie knows it would crush him, yet she finds it impossible to give up having other guys around.

What do all of these teens have in common? They are all experiencing unusually strong responses to feelings that are common to most people their age. Although many young people look at pornography, want to be in love, or peek at their neighbors, for some teens—like those described in this chapter—these types of sexual acts become an obsession, something that controls their lives, their schedules, and their relationships.

When Is Behavior a Problem?

There are many different kinds of sexual behavior, and society has very different views about people depending on their actions. For example, most people wouldn't worry about a teenage boy who frequently masturbates at home, but someone who consistently wants to spy on the neighbors would be labeled a Peeping Tom and would be considered threatening.

It's also possible to have a compulsive problem without acting on it. One of Mike's friends occasionally peeks at his neighbors naked, masturbates, and then goes on with his life without giving his behavior a second thought. But even if Mike never actually spies on anyone, being obsessed with the fantasy can be just as destructive to his mental health and social life as if he were hiding in the bushes with a pair of binoculars.

Not everyone who tries or even likes a particular practice will become addicted to it. And people who do

Many teens with sexual problems suffer in silence, feeling dirty and ashamed or thinking that they are alone.

something a lot aren't necessarily the ones for whom the act has the biggest impact. Later in the book, we'll discuss the signs and consequences of a behavior that has spiraled out of control.

Understanding Sex Addiction

Like a person with obsessive-compulsive disorder who constantly checks that the front door is locked or who washes his or her hands repeatedly, a person with sexual addiction is constantly and obsessively fantasizing about a sexual behavior, always trying to figure out when he or she will have the opportunity to do it again.

People with sexual compulsions are not freaks or perverts. Rather, they are some of the most lonely and confused teens. Their attempts to communicate are converted into dysfunctional sexual practices, which then make them feel even more alone and isolated.

There is also a lack of information for these young people about the causes of and treatments for their behaviors. Imagine saying to your mom, "I think I masturbate too much," or saying to a school counselor, "I'm worried that I'm addicted to pornography."

As a result, many of these young people suffer their problem alone, without ever realizing that they have a common disorder. Instead, they feel dirty and ashamed and think that they are the only person who has ever had such thoughts. If they don't get help, the behavior often continues and worsens.

The Dangers of Silence

Some sexual addicts will spend their whole lives in silence about their problem. They will always be worried about repressing their urges or hiding them and may shy away from making close friends and dating out of fear of what the other person will think of them.

Sometimes the behavior changes forms. Kids who constantly look at porn, for example, may grow up to visit prostitutes to get the same thrill. If the cost or safety becomes prohibitive, they may then go to strip bars instead. Many adults have lost thousands of dollars, immeasurable hours, and close friendships to fulfill sexual addictions.

Getting Help

These are sad losses, because sexual addictions are treatable. There are a number of options, from group therapy to prescription drugs, available to people suffering from sexual compulsion.

In the next few chapters, we'll discuss the technical definitions and types of compulsive sexual behavior, what differentiates a compulsive behavior from experimentation or a fantasy, how people's lives are affected by their behavior, and how treatment works.

Chapter Two

Defining Compulsive Sexual Behavior

When many people hear of sexual addiction, their first response is, "Is there such a thing? What's so bad about that?" But as you'll learn, whether their compulsion is seemingly normal or truly bizarre, people with obsessive sexual disorders are left feeling extremely lonely, depressed, and helpless about their situation. They are worlds apart from normal adults who enjoy active sex lives and can joke about being addicted to sex.

Mental Health Definitions

Psychologists and psychiatrists often disagree about what can be termed a sexual addiction. In fact, until about twenty years ago, sexual compulsions weren't even considered a psychological disorder; rather, they were viewed as perversions and personal choices.

Voyeurs are sexually stimulated by spying on people who do not realize that they are being watched.

Definitions among experts of acceptable behavior may differ depending on current social beliefs as well as their own personal values. For example, years ago a person engaging in satisfying, consensual homosexual sex would have been labeled a sexual deviant by most experts simply because same-sex relations were frowned upon by society.

Paraphilias and Nonparaphilias

The American Psychiatric Association (APA) distinguishes between paraphilias—fantasies or practices that lie outside the social norm—and nonparaphilias—behaviors that are considered normal.

The following are the seven most common paraphilic behaviors listed by the APA.

- Exhibitionists get sexual pleasure from exposing their genitals to an unsuspecting person or group. Exhibitionists generally choose a public place for their activities. Some experts believe the practice is as common among women as it is among men; however, it is rarely treated as a crime when it involves a female.

- Voyeurs are aroused by watching unsuspecting people who believe they are in a private situation. Voyeuristic acts can range from hiding videocameras in bathrooms and fitting rooms to spying on someone in his or her home as the person undresses or is intimate with another person. Many voyeurs are further turned on by the prospect of being caught.

- Masochists desire pain or the threat of pain from their sexual partners. While masochism is becoming a more commonly accepted practice among Americans when it occurs between two consenting adults, it can still be destructive. Masochists may be unable to experience pleasure in any other way and may go to more and more dangerous levels to achieve their wishes.

- Sadists wish to hurt or threaten their partners. Like masochism, experimenting with sadism is a growing part of today's sexual practices, but sadism itself can be very damaging. Sadists may

19

take out their urges on unsuspecting or unwilling partners. In some cases, the damage can go so far as to be considered assault or worse.

◆ Transvestic fetishism refers to a condition in which a person can become sexually aroused only when wearing (or holding) clothing associated with the opposite sex. The most common form of this behavior involves men wearing women's dresses, jewelry, makeup, and, particularly, undergarments. The activity is most damaging when it threatens an individual's self-definition or when it stays hidden from a partner.

◆ Frotteurism is the act of rubbing or fondling an unsuspecting stranger for sexual pleasure. The standard image of a frotteur is someone who enters a crowded street or bus and rubs against people in the group. Often the victims of this kind of act do not realize that they are being manipulated. If and when they do, that is another source of thrill for the frotteur, though it carries the risk of arrest and imprisonment.

◆ Pedophilia is a sexual attraction to young children, usually preadolescents. Pedophiles fantasize about having sexual or inappropriate relations with children who are too young to consent to sex acts. Pedophilia is one of the most damaging paraphilic behaviors. The act of pedophilia is always a crime—there is no way to legally act out pedophilic fantasies. It can result in long imprisonment for the perpetrator and a lifetime of pain for the victims and their families and friends.

Nonparaphilias

The four behaviors listed below are identified by the APA as compulsive but are usually considered part of normal human development and relations. Only when a person becomes obsessed with them are they labeled as disordered behavior. Remember, just because someone engages in these practices—no matter how often—doesn't mean that he or she is a sex addict.

- Fixation on an unattainable partner. To many, this is easily defined as an everyday crush gone very out of control. People may obsess about a celebrity or an attractive person they know. The fixation may lead the person to fantasize non-stop about the object of his or her desire, imagine a possible relationship with the person, base his or her moods and schedules on the person's actions, and sometimes even stalk the person.

- Compulsive masturbation. Many teens and even adults masturbate several times a day as part of their daily lives. With compulsive masturbation, however, the act becomes essential—compulsive masturbators may find themselves having to do it every two or three hours, stealing away into public bathrooms or secluded areas for privacy. Sometimes it becomes an outlet for dealing with stress, though ultimately it leads to increased anxiety about their behavior.

- Compulsive romantic relationships. Most commonly found among women, but certainly not uncommon in men, this compulsion leads people to become obsessed with a romantic ideal. They find one person after another and dive into passionate relationships that are often founded on very little substance. When the relationship invariably fails, they seek solace in their next romantic partner, whom they rely on to "save" or "fix" them.

- Compulsive sexuality in relationships. People who experience this pattern have an intense, immediate feeling that sex must be a part of any romantic relationship, regardless of the degree of emotional intimacy. They may go from partner to partner, having sexual intercourse as soon as possible with each new partner. The damage from this behavior often comes when the individual refuses to acknowledge other problems in the relationship,

People who feel that sex is the most important part of a relationship often neglect their partner's feelings.

addressing only issues that arise concerning sex. Such single-mindedness also may leave the romantic interest feeling objectified and unappreciated, seen only as a sexual partner by the other person.

What About Pornography?

Another commonly cited sexual addiction involves pornography. But looking at pictures and images of sex acts is usually just a socially and legally acceptable substitute for much more destructive behavior. Pornography is an easy, accessible outlet for people who feel some of the desires discussed above. Some compulsive masturbators become dependent on

Consuming pornography on a regular basis can lead to more dangerous sexual behaviors.

pornography to achieve pleasure. Pornographic material may be a paraphilic's only connection to his or her fantasy world. For example, a man who fantasizes about being tied up may find it more acceptable to look through certain pornographic magazines than risk telling his partner about his secret desires.

When Does Pornography Become Dangerous?

However, pornography can, and often does, lead to other, more dangerous sexually compulsive behaviors. Someone who usually settles for watching pornographic videotapes may eventually become so overwhelmed by his or her desires that he or she feels compelled to do something else when the opportunity presents itself: perhaps cheating on a partner when he or she meets someone new, or going to a prostitute when the urge to be with someone becomes so strong that the person becomes convinced that he or she can't live without sex.

"I view compulsive sexual behavior as an addictive process, so I focus on what function the behavior serves for the individual more than the specific sexual behaviors they choose," says Charles E. King, Ph.D., a clinical psychologist specializing in the treatment of compulsive sexual behavior who practices in Berkeley, California. "In fact, the people I have treated often have shifted among different behaviors over time. For example, they may frequent strip clubs or prostitutes, then shift to masturbating while viewing pornography on videos or the Internet because it seems less costly or less risky. But the underlying compulsion has not changed."

Who Suffers from These Addictions?

The frequency of certain behaviors often differs according to age and sex. For example, adults are likely to engage in affairs, while teenage disorders are often limited to pornographic addictions and masturbation. While teen males may find themselves using the Internet to view pornographic pictures, young women may use chat rooms, where they meet and begin relationships with a series of strangers.

Identifying a Problem

Some people may read the previous definitions and worry that they have a sexual compulsion because they masturbate often or daydream about dominating a sexual partner. George Deabill, Ph.D., a specialist in sexual addiction and sex therapy in California, says that by asking yourself a few simple questions, you can start to gauge whether your behavior is a normal sexual outlet or a potential problem: "Do you feel out of control? Are you taking high risks for your sexual thoughts? Do you feel okay? Is your thinking about sex interfering with your life, your schoolwork, your friendships? Many people think about sex a lot throughout their lives, and many male teens masturbate daily. What's going on in your life has to be understood before you can jump to the conclusion that you are an addict."

It's also true that very few teenagers are practicing sexual addicts. Experts believe that between 3 and 6 percent of Americans suffer from some form of compulsive sexual behavior. Most addictions don't blossom until people are in their twenties and thirties—until then, the behavior may be repressed, or take a milder or less threatening form. Teens whose sexual desires and behaviors make them feel depressed, isolated, or obsessed are the most likely to have their activity develop into a more destructive form of sexual practice.

Teenagers who have problems with sexual compulsion often access pornography via the Internet.

Sexual Addiction in Teens

"Teen sexual behavior is mostly limited by access," says Dr. King. "They are much less likely to get involved in commercial sexual enterprises because they don't have the money or transportation." King lists the following behaviors as the kind of sexual addictions most often experienced by adolescents:

- Use of phone sex and pornography in its many forms, accompanied by compulsive masturbation.

- Obscene phone calls, either to acquaintances or strangers. These may begin with "crank calls" and sometimes take on a sexual charge that

27

leads to the development of a compulsive pattern. These calls are not only unwelcome and distressing to the victims, but also illegal. Young people are often prosecuted for this kind of harassment.

◆ Secretly watching people undress.

◆ Getting into sexual relationships with older adults who then take advantage of them. The compulsive need for approval is often what leads teens into these exploitative situations.

◆ Prostitution, strip clubs, or other forms of using their bodies for money. Teens who have been sexually molested often feel that it is natural for them to "reenact" their exploitation by selling their bodies.

Chapter Three

What Is Normal?

Experts face several challenges when it comes to diagnosing the condition of sexual compulsion. The following are some of the complicated issues that make it very difficult to distinguish between normal and abnormal behavior.

Overpathologizing

This term means that in some cases, people are diagnosed with compulsive sexual behavior when their behavior is actually within the normal range. Often people seek psychological help after involvement in an affair or when they have been caught looking at pornographic materials by their partners. Many of these people are quick to diagnose themselves with a sexual addiction.

In fact, however, many of these people are experiencing a normal—though unpleasant—part of sexuality. Some dishonest doctors may encourage these people to believe that they have an illness in order to get money for treatment. It is important to remember that having sexual desires—even those that may seem unusual—is not the same as having a sexual disorder. Making a mistake in your personal life or in a relationship is not the same as having a disease.

Values Versus Diagnoses

For some people, their behavior falls within the realm of what is considered normal, but their personal values make them feel bad about it. Many men and women masturbate regularly and have sex before marriage. Even though these activities can be normal parts of human development, religious beliefs or moral values may make some people believe that they are perverts.

The shame and guilt patterns that arise when someone is acting against his or her core beliefs can lead to many of the same depressive, isolated feelings as compulsive sexual behavior. For these individuals, the most simple sexual behavior can result in a lack of self-respect, condemnation by their partners, depression, and withdrawal.

Whether a person is acting "normal" but feels overwhelming guilt, or has a more clinically defined sexual compulsion, anybody whose sexual behavior is causing

Strict religious beliefs may lead some people to believe that they are perverts.

them extreme guilt or is diminishing other aspects of their life can benefit from psychological help.

Routine Sexual Problems and Feelings

All of the conditions that are part of a sexual addiction can also exist without being part of a clinically diagnosed condition. For example, as already mentioned, many adolescents go through periods when they are obsessed with sex, even to the point of distraction.

In addition, young adults often go through periods when they have sexual relations with several partners over a short period of time. Within the category of paraphilic behaviors, many happy couples experiment

Despite the fact that most sex addicts are not dangerous to others, many feel lonely and shameful about their condition.

with minor forms of sadism or play-act other fantasies. Other sexually healthy people have secret fantasies their entire lives about exposing themselves or being dominated without ever telling anyone, acting on their desires, or experiencing any negative side effects.

Sometimes these things happen in phases—such as when a young woman sleeps with several men after a painful breakup but then stops, or a teenager who spends hours visiting pornographic Web sites over spring break, only to forget all about them once school has resumed. For other people, their sexual desires last a lifetime but never grow out of proportion. As we've said, unless a particular behavior or desire takes over a person's life, there's usually nothing to worry about.

Public Perception

Many people are strongly convinced that all sexual addicts are predators—criminals, perverts, offenders. In fact, experts say that fewer than 1 percent of sexual addicts are actually sexually violent or aggressive. Rather, most sex addicts feel lonely, sad, shameful, and embarrassed about their condition. Because of deep-seated notions of how a sex addict acts, however, many sufferers resist calling themselves compulsive—and suffer needlessly because they don't seek help.

How Does Obsessive Behavior Develop?

What is it that makes some people's deepest, secret desires grow into life-consuming obsessions? Dr. Patrick Carnes, one of the first researchers in sexual compulsion and still the foremost expert in the field, conducted an in-depth survey of sexual addicts and found that sufferers of sexual addiction have certain things in common.

History of Abuse

Abuse is common among people with compulsive sexual behavior. According to Dr. Carnes's study, 97 percent of patients reported that they had been emotionally abused as a child, 83 percent had been sexually abused, and 71 percent had been physically abused.

Psychologists theorize that being treated cruelly or being sexually molested leaves young people with a feeling of helplessness and guilt about sexuality. These feelings continue through their sexual development. As a result, any sexual feelings that these victims experience may make them feel bad, wrong, or dirty. Instead of working their desires into a healthy sex life, these people may feel the need to hide their urges or keep them separate from their "real" life. This starts a cycle of concealment and guilt about sexual feelings that may eventually become an addiction.

Victims of sexual abuse may also attempt to "recreate" their abuse through self-destructive behavior. They may take the power role and fantasize about being in control of sex, even going so far as to hurt others. They may also continually put themselves in the victim role, trying to relive their trauma in an attempt to feel victorious over it.

Lack of Communication

Children whose families do not discuss sex at all may be at risk for developing compulsions. Fearing that their sexual impulses are bad, teens in these families may hide their feelings—which may be completely normal—and create highly ritualized ways to act out their desires. These carefully constructed patterns then become the only way for the young person to express his or her sexuality.

Premature Sexuality

At the other end of the scale, families whose members talk very openly about sex may also contribute to a tendency toward sexual compulsion. A young person growing up in such a family may begin to overidentify too early with the sexual feelings and actions of an older family member. As a result, their premature behavior becomes a pattern. Instead of learning to develop nurturing and loving relationships, the person becomes overly focused on the sexual aspects of a partnership.

It is important to remember, however, that there are perfectly healthy people who come from both kinds of families. There is no reason to assume that one will become an addict simply because of the character of one's family.

Patterns of Other Behavioral Disorders

Carnes also found that over 40 percent of the patients interviewed also had problems with chemical dependencies, eating disorders, workaholism, compulsive spending, and gambling. This is further proof for experts that a sexual disorder is not simply a sexual abnormality but rather one sign of a much bigger life problem. A person who has trouble communicating with others may start drinking to increase his or her friendliness. To further decrease his or her loneliness, he or she might begin calling sex chat lines. The

It is common for people with sexual addiction to also have problems with drugs and/or alcohol.

drinking does not cause his or her sexual behavior; by the same token, sexual behavior does not lead to a problem with alcohol. Both behaviors are results of a serious problem with communication.

Other Factors

In the next chapter, we will take a closer look at how a need for intimacy, power, or release can create destructive sexual patterns.

Chapter Four

The Cycle of Compulsion

*A*drian, a high school junior, has had a terrible day. He was late for school, got in trouble with a teacher, and did poorly on a test he had forgotten to study for. Then a couple of guys in the cafeteria at lunch made fun of him, calling him a sissy.

Now that the day is finally over, he heads home and goes to his room. He logs onto the computer, knowing that he's probably going to look at some of his favorite pornographic sites. Last time he did this, his mom came home early and almost caught him. He was so scared that he swore he would never do it again. He even deleted his bookmarks.

But Adrian doesn't know what else to do—he feels frustrated, and nothing else works to get his mind off his problems like masturbating while looking at explicit images.

After he is done, Adrian feels terrible and guilty. What's wrong with me? he wonders. He is disgusted with himself and feels weak for having broken his promise not to look at the sites again. He hates the way he feels, and as he becomes more upset, he distracts himself by scrolling through more pictures. Soon he begins masturbating again, even though he wishes he weren't doing it.

Fifteen-year-old Jenny is grounded again. She missed her curfew again last night, and this time her mom happened to catch her. After a big fight, Jenny stormed into her room, and her mom said she wasn't allowed to be out past dinnertime for two weeks. Jenny waits until her mom has left for work in the morning, then calls her boyfriend, a sophomore at the local community college. She tells him that she wants to skip school and stay with him today, but he blows her off, saying that he has a big test he can't miss and plans with his friends.

Jenny feels rejected—first she gets in trouble for hanging out with this guy, and then he won't even make time for her. She thinks the problem must be her—guys don't ever seem to want to date her seriously after she has slept with them. Angry at her boyfriend and already late for school, Jenny heads to the diner near school where other students hang out when they are ditching

Sex addicts cannot manage their unpleasant emotions, which can lead them to act out in self-destructive ways.

school. She runs into Matt, a guy she made out with a few times the year before.

She tells Matt about her problems and he suggests that she needs a guy who really cares about how she feels. Matt invites Jenny to his house, where the two get drunk and wind up having sex. Jenny feels a little guilty for sleeping with another guy but is happy to be with someone who is finally listening to her.

How Does the Cycle Begin?

What makes an individual act on their sexual impulses instead of keeping them hidden? Why can't some people seem to stop themselves from doing things that are damaging, dangerous, or illegal? Mark Robinett, a marriage and family therapist in San Francisco, summarized the six steps that typically lead to a sexual compulsion.

1. Pain. The cycle begins when a person experiences something unpleasant. He or she may be stressed, nervous, angry, lonely, or even just bored. The person becomes upset and looks for ways to feel better but doesn't know how. He or she doesn't feel comfortable going to friends and loved ones for support, but they also feel unable to let go of the problem.

2. Dissociation. Dissociation happens when people aren't comfortable with the feelings they are having or the way they are handling an event, so they mentally and emotionally separate their identity from their behavior. People who dissociate may actually get to the point where when they are having unpleasant or anxiety-producing thoughts, they imagine that they are another person. They ignore their feelings and the stress in order not to feel guilty or disgusted by their behavior.

3. Altered state. Once the person dissociates, he or she continues doing things but does them in what is called an altered state. This means that

Dissociation resulting from extreme anxiety can cause a person to believe that he or she is someone else.

the person isn't acting as he or she usually would. They are not drunk or insane—they are simply behaving in a way that lets them deny their problems. Their desire to act out sexually becomes a way for them to feel better without actually addressing the real problem. For example, someone in an altered state who has had a fight with a partner might cheat instead of apologizing. The individual would feel better, even though he or she had actually done nothing to improve the relationship.

4. Pursuing. At this point, the person has decided on a form of sexual release to handle the problem

and makes an effort to begin the act. Pursuing refers to any act that helps a person find what they are looking for, from turning on the computer to find on-line pornographic images, to cruising for prostitutes, to going to a party to find a stranger to hook up with.

5. Behavior. This is the actual sexual act itself. It is often followed by feelings of guilt, shame, disappointment, emptiness, and regret—and often, at the same time, relief.

6. Repetition. Until this point, the process is just an act. It may be dysfunctional in that it does not deal with a problem directly. What makes the behavior compulsive, however, is that it happens repeatedly. Whether it is an hour later or six months later, the person will go through the same process the next time there is a situation that he or she feels incapable of handling. When the person continually and consistently reacts to situations with the particular behavior, he or she can be said to have compulsive sexual behavior or a sex addiction.

Sometimes the behavior is a quick activity that makes the person feel only a little bit better. More often, people repeat the behavior in increasingly extreme examples until they can make themselves feel totally different. Dr. Carnes found that 89 percent of sexual addicts "binge to exhaustion"—meaning that they commit their acts with such energy and emotion that they wind up too exhausted to deal with anything else.

Why Can't People Stop?

Why don't people just stop as soon as they realize that they are reenacting the same pattern? Robinett explains that breaking the cycle is not as easy as it may sound. Many people do not realize they are acting out sexually until they have reached step three, an altered state.

Once they feel divorced from their feelings, the next step is usually to act out. Because they are not in a normal frame of mind, however, they aren't as able to make a decision to stop the process. Instead, they go ahead with the behavior, feeling guilty and awful during it—but also not feeling that they have any alternative.

How Can the Cycle Be Broken?

In order to change their behavior, people have to realize at stages one or two that they are beginning the process. This requires sufferers to be self-aware. They must first figure out what triggers their behavior, whether it is sadness, loneliness, rejection, anger, frustration, or something else. Then the next time they experience one of these emotions, they must make a conscious effort to

To break the cycle of sex addiction, a person must learn to express feelings in more constructive ways.

express their feelings in a different way, such as talking to a friend, exercising, or having a good cry. Many people, though, instead dissociate without realizing it. Once they reach that point, it is too late to stop the process.

The challenge in overcoming compulsive sexual behavior is not stopping the act or the trigger, but changing the way that a person handles his or her life. An act itself, whether it is harmless masturbation or an illegal sexual act, is actually a result of something extremely upsetting in a person's life.

Could It Be Biological?

Some psychologists theorize that sexual addiction is actually a chemical addiction to adrenaline, a hormone made in the body. During a sex act, the excitement causes adrenaline to be released. The combination of the body's own biological rush and the psychological thrill of committing an illicit act makes people feel powerful, sexy, smart, and great about themselves. The "high" from getting away with hiring a prostitute or watching someone undress gives the person a sense of self-esteem. According to this theory, the person then gets addicted to this chemical and the behavioral rush it causes, and will continually aim for bigger and better highs.

Effects of Sexual Addiction

Whatever the mechanics, experts do agree that the process of sexually compulsive behavior has a series of effects on an individual's life. The person will start to organize his or her life around the next sexual release, constantly planning for or worrying about his or her next act. A porn addict might hoard certain magazines. A compulsive masturbator will schedule the day so that he or she can be in a bathroom at least every two hours. A man who goes to prostitutes will try for a high-paying job and create alibis for why he is not home every night. And a woman who wants to have sex with different guys will plan her nights so that she has the best chance of meeting new people.

As fantasizing about the behavior takes up more and more of the person's time, the behavior itself becomes ritualized. This means that the individual will have an exact idea of how, when, where, and why the behavior takes place. It may be a certain time of day or something that happens after every stressful conversation. But one thing is certain: It is definitely not a spur-of-the-moment decision. Addicts prepare for the act and know exactly how it will happen, even if they don't know why they're driven to do it.

Many addicts finish the act feeling guilty or ashamed, then soon find themselves wanting to do it "just one more time"—which, of course, repeats itself endlessly. Soon they are living a double life—the half that everyone knows about, and the other half, which indulges in the secret, hidden habits of sexual release.

Checklists

The following are some questions frequently used to determine whether someone has a sexual addiction. Although experts and organizations differ on some of the factors, they usually agree on some or all of these important points. Someone who answers yes to several of the following questions may be at risk for a sexual addiction. In the next chapter, we'll discuss types of resources available to sex addicts.

These questions were adapted from an outpatient program for sexual addiction.

1. Were you abused as a child?

2. Have you recently purchased or viewed pornographic materials?

3. Are you preoccupied with sexual thoughts?

4. Are your friends or loved ones worried about your behavior? Have they complained about you being preoccupied with sex?

5. Do you think you could stop your sexual behavior if you tried?

6. Has your sexual behavior created any problems for you?

7. Do you worry about people finding out about the nature or frequency of your sexual behavior?

8. Has your behavior emotionally hurt you or someone else?

9. Have you ever broken the law?

10. Do you feel bad about your sexual behavior?

11. Have you ever felt degraded by your sexual behavior?

12. Are you often depressed?

13. Do you have sexual relationships with people much older or much younger than you?

14. Do you feel like you're living a double or secret life?

15. Do you avoid sex?

16. After a sex act, do you want to get away from the person? Do you feel guilty, remorseful, or ashamed?

17. Have you ever tried to stop how frequently you masturbate, where you do it, or your fantasies?

18. Do you feel asexual or worry that you have no sexual feelings?

19. Do you feel like you're not a whole person if you're not having sex or in a relationship?

20. Do you pursue your sexual behavior so much that you don't pursue other areas of personal growth?

Dr. King offers a similar series of questions:

1. Have you had any concerns about your sexual behavior (in the last year)?

2. Have your lovers or friends been worried or upset about your sexual behavior?

3. Do you try to hide some of your sexual behavior from your friends and lovers?

4. Do you find it hard to keep commitments (to yourself or others) regarding your sexual behavior?

5. What do you wish to change about your sexual behavior?

6. What efforts have you made to change your sexual behavior?

7. What gets in the way of making these changes?

8. Do you have trouble stopping your sexual behavior when you know it is risky?

9. Have you ever felt that your sexual behavior was out of control?

10. Do you find yourself getting into more and more risky situations?

11. Is sex more exciting for you if there is some risk or danger involved?

12. What is important to you about sex? What does it do for you? How do you feel before, during, and after sexual episodes? How does it make you feel about yourself?

13. Do you count on sex as an escape or a way of coping with problems?

14. Do you ever feel like you are seeking a more perfect (or peak) sexual experience?

15. Do you feel that you have to be high (use drugs or alcohol) to have the sexual experience you want?

16. What would it be like for you to give up specific risky behaviors?

17. Have you had any STDs in the last year?

18. Has your sexual behavior caused you any problems? In your relationships? At school or work? With finances? With the law?

Chapter Five

Getting Help

Far from being something that happens only to other people, or something that doesn't really exist, sexual addiction is a real, serious illness that can strike anyone. It takes a tremendous toll on victims and those around them—financially, personally, and emotionally.

"The most common stereotype about sexual addicts is that they are creepy, seedy, ugly people," says Robinett. "The opposite is true. They're nice people, stuck on a road of sexual behavior that they can't seem to get off of. Look at Bill Clinton. He's a nice guy, trying to be likable, he wants to do the right thing. Yet, if the media is even half right about what has been reported, he's sexually out of control. He's the leader of the United States, but he's going to be remembered for his affairs."

Dr. King echoes those thoughts. "The public misconception is that people who engage in sexual misconduct are predatory, exploitive, and indifferent to the feelings of others," he says. "In fact, most of the people who seek treatment come with feelings of shame, sadness, and regret for the losses they have suffered and the harm they have caused others."

When Sexual Addicts Seek Treatment

What finally drives people with sexual compulsivity to seek professional help? Experts say that they are usually contacted after a person's partner finds out about the behavior and insists that the person get help. Another common motivation is an arrest or a close call. People who break the law may be forced to get help as part of their sentence, and people who are at risk of being caught may decide to finally stop their activities before they wind up in jail.

Dr. Carnes surveyed sex addicts and came up with the following list of problems commonly caused by compulsive sexual behavior.

- 72%: Suicidal thoughts

- 70%: Severe romantic problems

- 68%: Exposure to STDs, including AIDS

- 58%: Legal risks

- 40%: Loss of a partner or spouse

- 40%: Unwanted pregnancy

People with sexual problems may be made to feel guilty, when what they need is help and compassion.

- 36%: Abortions

- 27%: Career losses and problems

- 17%: Suicide attempts

People with compulsive sexual behavior may skip out on work, ignore loved ones, and not have time for relationships. People who find out that their partner engages in addictive behavior—affairs, prostitutes, looking at pornography, cross-dressing—often leave their partner out of disgust or anger. Controlled by their sexual behavior and seemingly unable to stop it, sexual addicts who seek help generally believe the following four statements.

- I am a bad person and unworthy of love.
- No one would love me if they knew what I did.
- Other people can't fulfill my needs, so I resort to these behaviors.
- Sex is my most important need.

Therapy and Support Groups

A popular option for sex addicts is to meet with a group of other sufferers. Sometimes the meetings are moderated by a professional and usually consist of addicts in varying stages of recovery. Some addicts find solace in religious-based therapy and group sessions. Usually a standard mission statement guides the meetings.

Some of the most popular programs in the United States include Sexaholics Anonymous, Sex and Love Addicts Anonymous, Sex Addicts Anonymous, and Sexual Compulsives Anonymous. All of them have their own definitions of acceptable behavior and different ways of achieving recovery.

Twelve-Step Programs

A majority of support groups (including all those listed above) are twelve-step programs. Modeled after the Alcoholics Anonymous method of recovery, participants meet regularly in group settings to share their experiences with their addictions. The twelve steps, when applied to sexual addiction, generally read something like the following:

1. We believe that we are powerless over our lust.

2. We believe in a greater power who can help us overcome our problem.

3. We turn ourselves over to a higher power for help.

4. We take a moral inventory of ourselves.

5. We admit our shortcomings.

6. We are ready to have a higher power remove our weaknesses.

7. We ask a higher power to forgive us.

8. We list the people who we've hurt and become ready to make amends.

9. We make amends with those we've hurt.

10. We continue to take inventory of our behavior and life.

11. We regularly pray and meditate to maintain our closeness with the higher power.

12. We carry the message of sexual recovery to others and practice our principles every day.

Therapy

Many addicts find help from professional counselors, psychologists, and psychiatrists. They may attend paid

Prescription drugs have successfully treated some sexual compulsivity.

group therapy sessions, where a professional leads a group dealing with several issues, or they may meet one-on-one with an expert. Psychologists focus on finding the root of compulsive sexual behavior and working with the individual to develop new skills for coping.

Prescription Drugs

Some sexual compulsivity has been successfully treated with prescription drugs. Anti-androgens lower the level of male testosterone in the body, and thus can lower a person's libido. More recently, a family of anti-depressants called SSRIs (selective serotonin reuptake inhibitors), including Prozac, Zoloft, and Paxil, have been shown to decrease sexually compulsive behavior in some people. These drugs act on the level of serotonin in the brain—a hormone that controls moods, including obsessive thoughts, anxiety, and depression.

A Lifelong Struggle

For most addicts, the struggle with sexual compulsion will be a lifelong battle. At every turn and bend of the road, they will find themselves tending toward the same behaviors that caused them countless problems in the past. Many will relapse and temporarily give up hope of a recovery. For the most unfortunate, the behavior will continue until it has destroyed their lives.

For most, though, the uphill path to recovery is well worth the effort. Although retraining themselves to deal with life and their sexual impulses is difficult, its effects are priceless. Learning to cope isn't just about stopping a compulsive sexual behavior, it's about finding out how to be involved in meaningful, mutually beneficial, honest, mature relationships.

"For anyone worried about whether they have a sexual addiction, I think common sense is a good starting point," says Robinett. "It's very normal for a teen to think about sex nonstop and masturbate frequently. But if you're doing anything stupid, dangerous, or illegal to get your sexual thrills—putting date rape drugs in people's drinks, assaulting people, on-line four hours a day, anything excessive—then surely it's worth seeking help."

Glossary

compulsion   An unstoppable urge to engage in certain behavior.

compulsive sexual behavior   Repetitive, cyclical and destructive sexual practices—may be paraphilic or nonparaphilic.

exhibitionism   Psychological desire to expose one's genitals to an unsuspecting person.

frotteurism   Psychological desire to rub up against or otherwise touch an unsuspecting person.

masochism   Psychological desire to be harmed by another individual.

nonparaphilic compulsions   Common sexual practices that become problematic when a person begins to obsess over and ritualize them.

paraphilia   A sexual practice or desire that involves an unusual element like a nonliving object or a

situation in which one partner has no power. A
medical and legal term for deviance.

pathologizing The act of labeling a certain behavior as a medically recognized disorder.

pedophilia Psychological desire to involve young
children in sexual activity.

pornography Graphic pictures, video, film, writing,
and/or speech that depicts sexual relations in
order to sexually arouse the reader or viewer.

ritualize To create a specific set of behaviors leading up to, following, and related to an act.

sadism Psychological desire to inflict pain.

sexual addict An individual whose relationship with
sex has negatively overshadowed other aspects of
his or her life and who cannot stop the behavior.

sexual offender A person whose sexual behavior
breaks the law.

transvestic fetishism Psychological desire to
wear clothing of the other gender; cross-dressing
for pleasure.

trigger An event that causes a person to feel sad,
lonely, angry, confused, or stressed; in sexual
addicts, the event may begin a chain reaction that
results in the sexual behavior.

voyeurism Psychological desire to watch an
unsuspecting person, usually in a state of undress
or intimacy.

Where to Go for Help

In the United States

National Council on Sexual Addiction and Compulsivity
1090 Northchase Parkway, Suite 200
South Marietta, GA 30067
(770) 989-9754
Web site: http://www.ncsac.org/html/main.html

Online Sexual Addiction
P.O. Box 13602
San Luis Obispo, CA 93406
Web site: http://www.onlinesexaddict.com

Sex Addicts Anonymous (SAA)
P.O. Box 70949
Houston, TX 77270
(800) 477-8191
Web site: http://www.sexaa.org

Sexaholics Anonymous (SA)
P.O. Box 111910
Nashville, TN 37222-1910
(615) 331-6230
Web site: http://www.sa.org

Sex and Love Addicts Anonymous (SLAA)
P.O. Box 338
Norwood, MA 02062-0338
(781) 255-8825
Web site: http://www.slaafws.org

Sexual Compulsives Anonymous (SCA)
Old Chelsea Station
P.O. Box 1585
New York, NY 10011
(212) 439-1123
(800) 977-HEAL
Web site: http://www.sca-recovery.org

In Canada

Sex and Love Addicts Anonymous (SLAA) Canada
300 Coxwell Avenue
Box 22514
Toronto, ON M4L 2A0
(416) 486-8201

Web Sites

Mayo Clinic—Compulsive Sexual Behavior
http://www.mayohealth.org/mayo/9708/htm/sex_obse.htm

SexHelp.com
http://www.sexhelp.com

Sexual Addiction Help
http://www.sexaddicthelp.com

Sexual Addiction Recovery Resources
http://home.rmi.net/~slg/sarr

Sexual Recovery Institute
http://www.sexualrecovery.com

For Further Reading

Carnes, Patrick J. *Out of the Shadows: Understanding Sexual Addiction.* Chicago: Hazelden Information Education, 1992.

———. *Don't Call It Love: Recovery from Sexual Addiction.* New York: Bantam, 1992.

Halpern, Howard M. *Finally Getting It Right: From Addictive Love to the Real Thing.* New York: Bantam, 1995.

Hastings, Anne Stirling. *Treating Sexual Shame: A New Map for Overcoming Dysfunction, Abuse, and Addiction.* Northvale, NJ: Jason Aronson, 1998.

Schaumburg, Harry W. *False Intimacy: Understanding the Struggle of Sexual Addiction.* Colorado Springs, CO: NavPress, 1997.

Index

About the Author

Laura Gilbert has worked as an editor and writer for *Cosmopolitan* and *Fitness* magazines. She lives in Brooklyn, New York.

Photo Credits

Cover by Ira Fox. All interior shots by Kristen Artz.

Layout

Geri Giordano